SOLVING
SCIENCE
MYSTERIES

Why Do Volcanoes Erupt?

All About Earth Science

Nicolas Brasch

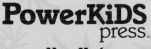

PowerKiDS
press.

New York

Published in 2010 by The Rosen Publishing Group, Inc.
29 East 21st Street, New York, NY 10010

Produced and designed by Denise Ryan & Associates
Editor: Helen Moore and Edwina Hamilton
Designer: Anita Adams
Photographer: Lyz Turner-Clark
U.S. Editor: Kara Murray

Photo Credits: p4 top: Copyright: Jim Lopes; p4 middle: Michael Chambers; p4 bottom: © Photographer: Amelia Takacs | Agency: Dreamstime.com; p5 top: © Photographer: Ricardo Saraiva | Agency: Dreamstime.com; p5 middle: Robb Kiser; p5 bottom: © Photographer: Jubalharshaw19 | Agency: Dreamstime.com; p6 bottom: Fotolibra; p7 top: Valerie Koch; p8 top: Terry Wilson; p8 second from top: Steffen Foerster; p8 third from top: Don Wilkie; p8 bottom: Gary Milner; p9: Getty Images/Thomas Cranmer; p10 top: David Ritter; p10 bottom left: Don Bayley; p10 bottom right: Lawrence Sawyer; p11 bottom: © Photographer: Cristian Nitu | Agency: Dreamstime.com; p12 top: © Photographer: Ron Sumners | Agency: Dreamstime.com; p12 bottom: © Travis Manley | Dreamstime.com p13 top right © Photographer: David Pruter | Agency: Dreamstime.com; p13 middle: Jan van der Hoeven; pps 14 middle and bottom, 16 top, p17 bottom, 18 top and 19 bottom: Photolibrary; p15 bottom left: © Photographer: Gautier Willaume | Agency: Dreamstime.com; p15 right: © Photographer: Cj Yu | Agency: Dreamstime.com; p17 top: State Library of Victoria; p18 bottom DK Images; p19 top: Rade Lukovic; p20: Sascha Beck.

Library of Congress Cataloging-in-Publication Data

Brasch, Nicolas.
  Why do volcanoes erupt? : all about earth science / Nicolas Brasch.
    p. cm. — (Solving science mysteries)
  Includes index.
  ISBN 978-1-4488-0400-9 (lib. bdg.) — ISBN 978-1-4488-0401-6 (pbk.) —
ISBN 978-1-4488-0402-3 (6-pack)
  1. Geology—Miscellanea—Juvenile literature. 2. R ocks—Miscellanea—Juvenile literature. I. Title.
  QE29.B695 2010
  551.21—dc22

                    2009038258

Manufactured in the United States of America

CPSIA Compliance Information: Batch #WW10PK: For Further Information contact Rosen Publishing, New York, New York at 1-800-237-9932

Contents

 Questions About Rocks Through the Ages 4

Questions About Rocks and Violent Activity . . . 6

Questions About Rocks and Mining 8

Questions About Rocks and Growth 10

It's a Fact 12

Can You Believe It? 14

Who Found Out? 16

It's Quiz Time! 20

Try It Out! 22

Glossary 23

Index and Web Sites 24

Questions About Rocks Through the Ages

Q: Why do rocks change shape?

A: Rock formations are changed by wind, water, and ice. This process is known as weathering or **erosion**. Cliffs are formed by the constant smashing of waves against a coastline, while wind can make holes in rock formations so that they become caves. However, it usually takes millions of years of erosion for a landscape to change dramatically.

eroded landscape

Q: What is a fossil?

A: A fossil is the remains or the **impression** of something that lived long ago. Most fossils are found in rocks. Fossils are formed when the remains or impression of a living thing settles in mud or another soft substance that later forms into a rock. The rock encloses and protects the remains or impression so that it lasts for thousands, or even millions, of years.

fish fossils

Questions About Rocks and Violent Activity

Q: How are mountains formed?

A: Earth is made up of a series of platelike slabs of rock. These are known as tectonic plates. Some of the plates carry the continents, while others carry the oceans. The plates that carry the continents are called continental plates. When two continental plates collide, massive amounts of earth are forced upward to become mountains.

Continental plates collide to force earth upward to form mountains.

Q: Why do volcanoes erupt?

A: A volcano is a **vent** in Earth's surface. Heat is constantly melting rocks inside Earth. These melted rocks are known as lava. A volcanic eruption occurs when **molten** lava bursts through a vent in Earth's crust. While lava can be more than 1,832° F (1,000° C) inside the planet, as soon as it hits the outside atmosphere, it cools. When it has completely cooled, it turns into rock again.

The Volcanic Explosivity Index

Index	Description	Height	Volume	How often
0	Nonexplosive	< 330 feet (100 m)	< 35,000 ft^3 (1,000 m^3)	Daily
1	Gentle	330–3,300 ft (100–1,000 m)	> 350,000 ft^3 (10, 000 m^3)	Daily
2	Explosive	1–3 mi (1–5 km)	> 35,000,000 ft^3 (1,000,000 m^3)	Weekly
3	Severe	2–9 mi (3–15 km)	> 350,000,000 ft^3 (10,000,000 m^3)	Yearly
4	Cataclysmic	6–16 mi (10–25 km)	> 3,500,000,000 ft^3 (100,000,000 m^3)	10s of years
5	Paroxysmal	> 16 mi (25 km)	> .2 mi^3 (1 km^3)	100s of years
6	Colossal	> 16 mi (25 km)	> 2 mi^3 (10 km^3)	100s of years
7	Supercolossal	> 16 mi (25 km)	> 24 mi^3 (100 km^3)	1,000s of years
8	Megacolossal	> 16 mi (25 km)	240 mi^3 (1,000 km^3)	10,000s of years

The Volcanic Explosivity Index measures the explosiveness of volcanic eruptions.

Questions About Rocks and Mining

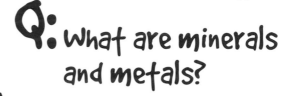

native copper

gold

silver

Q: What are minerals and metals?

A: Minerals are **compounds** that are formed by rocks changing under heat and pressure. They are found within rocks and include coal and iron ore. Metals are a type of mineral. Copper, gold, and zinc are examples of metal. Minerals are obtained by mining, which involves removing them from rocks using machines made for that purpose.

Q: What are the Rockies?

A: The Rockies are the Rocky Mountains, a major mountain range in western North America. They stretch for over 3,000 miles (4,828 km) from New Mexico through Colorado, Wyoming, and Montana and north across the Canadian border. They form a natural border between the Canadian provinces of British Columbia and Alberta and end in the **boreal** forests of northern British Columbia. The Rockies are rich in deposits of copper, iron ore, silver, gold, lead, zinc, phosphate, potash, and gypsum. The Wyoming Basin and a number of smaller areas also contain coal, natural gas, oil shale, and petroleum.

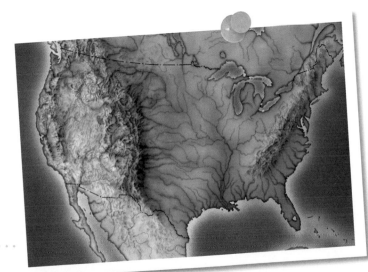

Questions About Rocks and Growth

Q: How do lichens survive by living on rocks?

A: Lichens are a type of plant. Some of them grow on trees but many of them grow on rocks. They are able to live on rocks because they obtain much of their nourishment from the air. They also obtain minerals directly from the rocks. Another advantage is that lichens are part **algae**, which means they can make food for themselves from gases in the atmosphere.

lichen growing on rocks

Q: What is the difference between a stalactite and a stalagmite?

A: Stalactites and stalagmites are naturally formed structures that are found in limestone caves. They are formed by dripping water. When the drops of water **evaporate**, the minerals in the water form a solid structure. When this structure hangs from the ceiling of the cave, it is known as a stalactite. When this structure forms a column from the ground, it is known as a stalagmite.

stalactite

stalagmite

It's a Fact

> Formation of the Himalayas
The Himalayas are mountains that were formed about 50 million years ago, when the Indian and Eurasian continental plates crashed into each other.

> Shimmering Sapphire
Sapphire, which is the second-hardest natural substance in the world, is mined in many countries including Brazil and the United States. Sapphires are usually blue but they can also be green, yellow, gold, or purple.

> The Stone Age
The Stone Age is a period in history when humans used stones as tools. This period may have begun several million years in the past and lasted up until about 15,000 years ago.

> Pangaea
All the continents on Earth were once one gigantic continent known as Pangaea. Pangaea started splitting up about 220 million years ago.

> The Largest Monolith

A monolith is a single block of rock. The largest monolith in the world is Mount Augustus, in western Australia. Mount Augustus is 5 miles (8 km) long and covers 18.5 square miles (47.95 sq km).

> Mount Rushmore

The huge sculptures of four American presidents carved in the rock of Mount Rushmore were created by artists and laborers using dynamite and jackhammers.

Mount Augustus, western Australia

Types of Rocks

There are three types of rocks: igneous, sedimentary, and metamorphic. Igneous rocks are formed when molten lava cools. Sedimentary rocks are created when layers of tiny particles of sand and stone build up over millions of years. Metamorphic rocks are formed when igneous or sedimentary rocks undergo extreme heat or pressure.

Mount Rushmore, South Dakota

Can You Believe It?

Rocks from Space

Scientists have learned a great deal about Earth, our solar system, and the universe by studying rocks from space. Some of these rocks have landed on Earth as meteorites, while others have been brought back to Earth by spacecraft. Studies of Moon rocks and the Moon's surface led scientists to believe that the Moon was once a part of Earth.

Dating Rocks

Geologists use a process known as **radioactive** dating to work out how old rocks are. Rocks contain radioactive elements that decay over time. Geologists know the amount of radioactive elements that different types of rock have and they know the rate at which this decay occurs. By finding out the current amount of radioactive elements in a rock, they can calculate when the rock was formed.

The Terra-cotta Soldiers

In the Chinese city of Xi'an is a series of pits containing about 8,000 life-size figures of soldiers made from **terra-cotta**. The were ordered by Emperor Qin Shi Huang and sculptured just over 2,000 years ago. The emperor had the soldiers positioned around the tomb he was to be buried in. He wanted them to protect his tomb from invaders.

Who FoUnd out?

Father of Modern Geology: James Hutton

The Scottish geologist James Hutton (1726–1797) is sometimes referred to as the founder of **geology**. He originally studied medicine but later turned to geology. His observations of cliffs and mountains led him to question the established belief that rocks were formed by the actions of water. Hutton's findings led him to believe that rocks were formed by intense heat and pressure from within the planet. This idea became known as the Plutonian theory and is the basis of modern geology.

Geologist: Edgeworth David

Sir Tannatt William Edgeworth David (1858–1934) was a Welsh-born Australian geologist. In 1907 he led a party, which included Douglas Mawson, on the first successful attempt to climb an active volcano, Mount Erebus, which is 12,447 feet (3,794 m) tall, in Antarctica. With two others he then trudged over 1,260 miles (2,028 km) of ice and snow to be the first to reach the South Pole. Edgeworth David also discovered the Hunter Valley coalfield, a major coal deposit. His contribution to Australian geology was, and continues to be, unequalled.

Mount Erebus, Antarctica

17

One Giant Continent: Alfred Wegener

The German geologist Alfred Wegener (1880–1930) is considered to be the first person to suggest that all the continents on Earth had once been joined together. He gave this supercontinent the name Pangaea, which means "all earth." He also claimed, correctly, that the continents were still moving and always would move. He called this **phenomenon** continental drift. Unfortunately, Wegener's explanation as to why the continents were drifting was incorrect. As a result, scientists dismissed his theories about continents for about 50 years. Later it was found that Wegener had been correct about continental drift.

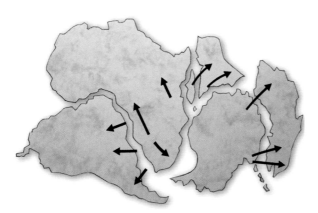

this is how Earth's continents started to drift apart 250 million years ago

Physicist: Hans Geiger

The German **physicist** Hans Geiger (1882–1945) was the coinventor of the Geiger counter. His colleague was the New Zealand-born physicist Ernest Rutherford. They invented the first Geiger counter in 1908, but Geiger made improvements to it over the next two decades. The Geiger counter is a device that measures the type and amount of **radiation** in an object. By determining the type and amount of radiation in a rock, geologists can figure out how old the rock is.

It's Quiz Time!

The pages where you can find the answers are shown in the red circles, except where otherwise noted.

Find the odd one out

1. daffodil   rose   lichen   geranium   (10)

2. stalagtite   stalagmite   dripping water   koala   (11)

3. borglum   igneous   sedimentary   metamorphic   (13)

Choose the correct words

1. The Rockies are rich in (banks, stands, deposits) of copper, iron ore, silver, gold, lead, zinc, phosphate, potash, and gypsum.   (9)

2. The tectonic plates that carry the continents are called (continental, oceanic, Wegener) plates.   (6)

3. The largest monolith in the world is Mount (Everest, Kilimanjaro, Augustus).   (13)

Rock of Ages crossword

Across

1. Remains of something that lived long ago ⑤

4. Rocks formed when molten lava cools ⑬

5. A vent in Earth's surface ⑦

7. An Australian rocky formation ⑬

Down

2. A period in history ⑫

3. A hanging structure in limestone caves ⑪

4. A single, huge block of rock ⑬

6. Someone who studies rocks ㉓

Try It Out!

Reread page 7 about volcanoes. Now let's make our own volcano and watch it erupt!

What You'll Need:

- empty bottle, large dish, baking soda, vinegar, dish soap, red food coloring, a measuring cup, and a spoon

What to Do:

1. Put the empty bottle inside the large dish. Use the spoon to fill the bottom of the bottle with baking soda.
2. Pour some vinegar in your measuring cup. Add two drops of dish soap and of food coloring. Stir it with your spoon.
3. Now pour the vinegar mixture into the bottle that has the baking soda. What happens?

Now Try This!

Read about the different kinds of rocks on page 13 again. Rocks are always changing. This is called the rock cycle. Look up the rock cycle on the Internet or at the library. Then make a cycle chart that shows the different steps in the rock cycle.

Glossary

algae (AL-jee) A type of plant or plantlike organism with no flowers.

boreal (BOR-ee-ul) Toward or located in the north.

cataclysmic (KA-tuh-kliz-mik) Having to do with a violent natural event.

compounds (KOM-powndz) Things made up of two or more elements.

erosion (ih-ROH-zhun) Wearing away.

evaporate (ih-VA-puh-rayt) To disappear into the air.

geologists (jee-AH-luh-jists) Scientists who study Earth's structure.

geology (jee-AH-luh-jee) The science that deals with Earth's structure.

impression (im-PREH-shen) Mark or imprint.

molten (MOHL-ten) Made liquid by heat.

paroxysmal (pa-ruk-SIZ-mul) Sudden or violent.

phenomenon (fih-NO-meh-non) Occurrence or happening.

physicist (FIH-zuh-sist) Someone who studies physics (the way things act and react).

radiation (ray-dee-AY-shun) The production of energy as electromagnetic waves.

radioactive (ray-dee-oh-AK-tiv) Producing radiation energy in the form of rays, waves or particles.

terra-cotta (ter-uh-KO-tuh) A form of clay made from earth.

vent (VENT) An outlet.

Index

C
compounds, 8
continents, 6, 12, 18

E
Earth, 6–7, 12, 14, 18
erosion, 4
eruption, 7

F
fossil(s), 5

G
Geiger, Hans, 19

geologist(s), 14, 16–19
geology, 16–17

I
ice, 4, 17
impression, 5

L
landscape, 4

P
phenomenon, 18

R
radiation, 19

remains, 5
rock formations, 4
rock(s), 5–8, 10, 13–14, 16, 19

T
tectonic plates, 6
terra-cotta, 15

V
vent, 7

W
water, 4, 11
waves, 4
wind, 4

Web Sites

Due to the changing nature of Internet links, PowerKids Press has developed an online list of Web sites related to the subject of this book. This site is updated regularly. Please use this link to access the list:

www.powerkidslinks.com/ssm/erupt/